Bows and Arrows, Homemade

A pictorial guide

Copyright © 2011 Paul Carpenter

Learn how to make

a long Bow

a flat bow

Plus the all important arrows and bow string

Published by Lulu.com

ISBN number 978-1-4709-4008-9

Other publications by Paul Carpenter

Travel;

Six Mountain hikes from around the World

The Moray way and the Ben Macdui Trail

Crafts;

Leather and Wood Crafts

The leather lace Bullwhip

Leather Armour

Leather Projects

Contents

Make a Long Bow from staves   5

Including: tools, marking out, roughing out, tillering, final tiller and backing.

With an introduction to tanning and dying rawhide.

Make a Flat Bow from Timber   23

Including: selection of wood, marking out, initial floor tillering, backing with rawhide, final tiller and polish.

With ideas for other backing methods for weak spots or when using soft wood.

Make Arrows and String   41

Including: shaft sizes, making the nock, paint/decoration, points, different fletch and how to attach them.

String jig, setting up string, making end loops/serve, reverse twist dacron string.

Resources   63

As always, the procedures outlined within this book you do at your own risk.

Caution – if you do use axes, power tools and other potentially dangerous tools, make sure you know how to use them i.e. how to stand/hold/cut with them – it's the wood your trying to cut not you or anybody else – use of apparatus (which make bow making easier and safer) such as shave Horse.

Making a long bow from staves

Making bows with timber or staves that you have cut down and dried for a year or bought is possibly one of the greatest ways to make a bow – it is essentially a naturally laminated bow of sap and heart wood made the way you want it like people all over the world have been doing since time began. I call these self bows because of that, although some call them long bows. I say call it what you want, you made it.

What most should agree on is that naturally dried wood, as opposed to heat dried wooden timbers retains alot more of its strength per similar volume to timbers because the cells and fibres are not damaged as much.

Tools, marking and roughing out, then tillering, backing finishing with two short pieces about tanning and dyeing of rawhide.

Figure 1

This is a 50lb yew bow (low altitude grown yew) and when first made could shoot an arrow to 160m but I have made bows out of mountainous American white ash and Osage orange which were longer and of narrower profile that could easily out shoot that distance (gotta make sure you're in a really big field when testing these bows!!).

Figure 2

Tools - Gransfors axes are quite expensive but they are sharp and keep their edge very well, although other axes would do. The drawknife I use has a very thin blade unlike many others I've got and seems to allow me more control while cutting. Lastly the shaving horse is possibly the best bit of gear for self bow making, a perfect third hand positioning the bow at the right angle – plans for these can be found in **Google** land.

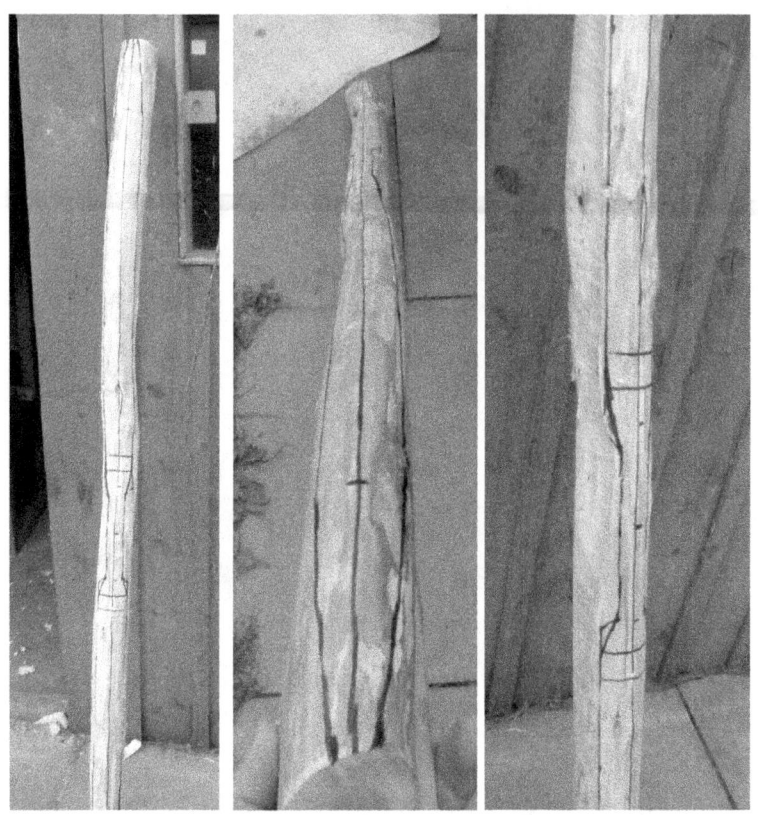

top profile

side profile

I mostly make what is either called a long bow or self bow depending on your opinion - their both basically the same as the dimension cut are gradual from nock to handle - basically 6 foot long, 1 1/2 - 2 inches at handle and 1/3 - 1/2 inch at nocks and cut in a D shape profile with slight bend (or none at all) at handle.

Marking

Yew staves are hard to come by these days and expensive to buy but if you ask your local tree surgeon, if they don't have yew they probably have loads of other woods you could use. If you buy a stave they are probably already dried and cut to rough dimensions. Staves from a tree surgeon will need to be split. Avoid trunks that have a twist in them, what you're looking for is fairly straight trunks with very few branches or knots of a slow grown tree about 1 foot in diameter with sap wood under 5 – 6mm thick. After splitting, quarter and remove the bark then on the bare sap wood mark out the outline of your bow as shown on the previous page. These marks are just a rough outline to aid in your removal of wood; the actual finish dimension will be slightly less. Remember to leave an inch either end of the stave. The stave shown has a slight twist in it around the handle area but the nocks do match up – it produced a nice 55lb bow @ 29 where the bowstring was naturally off centre at the handle.

Figure 3

Roughing out — Both Figures 3 and 4 show different stages in the removal of wood — <u>Start</u> with the camp and mini hatchets to rough cut the stave to just above your dimension lines starting from the handle downwards — it is advisable to rest the stave on a chopping block as you near the nocks to protect the axe blade. Be careful as ever and take your time, chopping and looking at the stave now and again, plus make sure you are standing properly and well balanced — cut the wood not yourself or anyone else. <u>Next</u> the stave should now fit into the shaving horse clamp — starting at the handle again use the drawknife to shave the wood down to the dimension lines and create a rectangular profile of the stave. If the stave has thick sap wood, you will need to shave that down as well to roughly 5mm thick — the power of a bow is in the heart wood so leaving too much sap will produce a very weak bow.

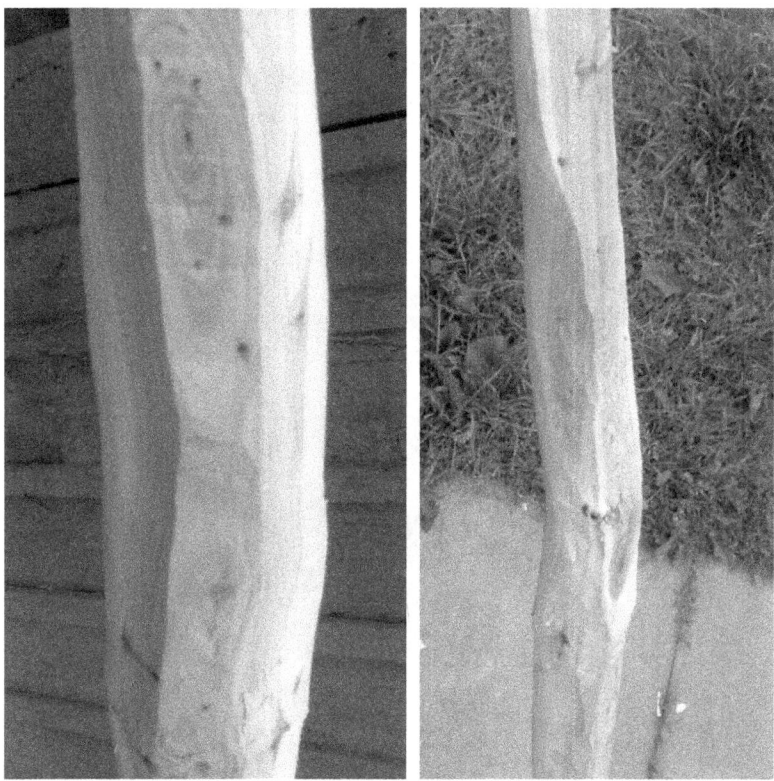

Figure 4

Figure 5

Floor Tillering

— After shaving down to the dimension lines, you next start creating the D profile and handle. Start shaving away at the sides as shown in figure 4, drawing a guide line from sap side up about 5mm helps. Next shave away at the belly of the bow leaving the area around the handle slightly raised unless you want it to bend there as well – as you do this stage remember to keep taking out the stave and floor testing it as shown in figure 5. What you are doing in this stage is cutting to final dimension lines and roughing out the general profile of the limbs and shaving away only enough wood to start a slight bend as shown above right. Once this is achieved, you can either go onto final tillering or back it. In both instances, the stave should be shaved down to its final dimensions.

Backing — Backing a bow which has a curved back side is very different to a flat one as shown above. The rawhide should be cut slightly larger than the bows dimensions and wetted. Glue both the belly of the bow and rawhide. Allow both to dry then place rawhide on using a scraper to remove any air bubbles carefully. I use strips of wetted rawhide wrapped around the bow to aid keeping it in place which should tighten as it dries, meaning I don't have to try and keep it tight as I wind it on which is very awkward to do. I normally leave this on for a couple of days, then remove the wrapping and trim the rawhide. If you use very thick rawhide like over 2mm thick you may have to floor tiller the bow again.

Tillering — (leave tillering till a week after backing is applied) The final stage of tillering is the most skilled part of making a self bow and involves using two pieces of essential equipment. First being a solid thin, long piece of wood with grooves cut out of it at spaces of 1 inch starting from 10 inches from the end to 30 inches. The second should include (but not shown) a wide, thin piece of wood with U shape cut out of the top of it attached 5 -6 feet up a wall (wide enough to accommodate the handle of a bow and deep enough to ensure it stays in place) with a pulley attached in the same wall directly underneath it at just above floor level (a marked grid on the wall behind helps to judge curve). Plus I use what I call a tillering string which is made extra thick from Dacron (24 ply instead of 12). The stick is mainly an aid when testing strength of bow by setting up as shown then without releasing the string from the groove taking the strain of it with a weighting devise of some sort (I use the kind fisherman use with a hook one end) . Plus it serves to help you to look at the bow more carefully to judge it's tiller or even take photos of it. The pulley devise is where most of the work occurs. After the floor tiller is over, attach the tillering string and place the bow in the wood fixed into the wall, then attach another string from that string directly underneath the centre of the bow, play it through the pulley and walk back. The purpose of this is so you can first pull the bow a few times (allowing the bow to compensate for any wood removed) and judge where any needs to be removed. In the photo above it is obvious that although the right limb is fairly even in the way it bends, the left one bends more near the handle then has no bend from the mid section to the nock – you only remove wood where it does not bend, so it would mean that a little should be removed from the left mid section to the nock. When I say a little, I mean that you may have to only use sand paper, definitely don't use an axe or the drawknife. The most essential thing to do is re-test the tiller after every small piece of wood removed. It takes time and you may ruin it a few times, I did and still do after not making one for awhile. You test the tiller all the way from strung to 30 inches.

Sanding/Polishing

When you're happy with the tillering, the bow can have its final sanding. I use very fine 180 grit then wet the bow and run the wire wool over it repeating this about three times (this gets rid of very fine fibres) then I rub a stone over it all (except for the back – leave this semi rough to take the backing if you want one) which serves to compound the wood after the wetting and brings the wood upto a very nice sheen. Once the bow is tillererd and smoothed, paint on some varnish (I use yacht varnish) to avoid the rawhide getting damp. Apply about three coats sanding down each with the wire wool – this will then produce a smooth surface.

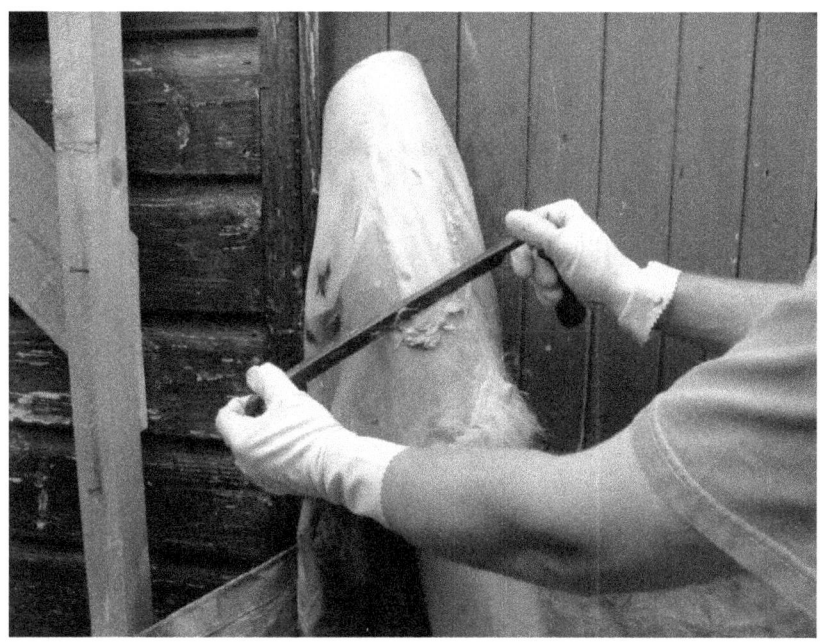

Tanning Rawhide — Tanning your own rawhide creates great satisfaction but is also very hard and smelly work but I guess mostly the cost is alot less than buying them. I get my deer skins from a local game supplier and cow hides from a local farmer, both arrive normally the same day they were skinned but sometimes salted. My equipment includes a thick bladed drawknife blunted by a stone, an old piece of drainage pipe roughly 15cm in diameter, a dustbin of about 120litres capacity and stretching frame about 6 foot by 5.5 feet. Depending on the time of year, the hides you get may be covered in huge ticks or have holes where an insect eggs have hatched, you can freeze the hide to kill the ticks, as for the holes just be careful around them when you scrape the hide to ensure you don't make them any bigger. First job is to remove fat and meat from the back of the hide as shown above, this tends to be easier if the hide was salted but if not it can be still quite wet, greasy and slippery. Second, if the hide is not salted, then salt it on the hair side with the type of salt they use on roads and roll up and leave for a couple of day (the heat produced starts the bacterial reaction needed to separate the epidermis from the skin). <u>Third</u> place the hide into the dustbin and soaks with water, if you have not removed all the fat and meat the hide will fester in the water and start stinking really badly in a few days. There are chemicals and kits you can buy for this stage which when added into the water speed up the process needed to remove the hair easily but after using them I tend to find just the water and salt does the trick. The trouble with chemicals is that you need to soak the hide in running water after it is de-haired so that those chemicals come out. After about 3 days I start testing the hide and seeing how easily the hair comes off, normally after 4 they should ready. <u>Lastly</u> place the hid onto the drainage beam again and remove the hair – this can be hard around the neck and back where the hide is thickest to easy around the sides. Once all hair is removed trim the hide to fit the frame, make holes along the edge of the hide (I used an old blunt awl) then tie onto frame starting at the top going around either side. One time I had five hides going on at the same time and just nailed each onto the side of my shed – as long as they are placed somewhere windy or in the sun and stretch tight they should dry quite quickly. Once dry use a sharp knife to cut them out close to the edges then roll up (or leave flat if thick cowhide) and store somewhere dry and dark.

Dying Rawhide

– I use numerous materials for dyes from tree bark, grass and nettle leaves plus other that can be bought, but mostly use what's around me – experiment with anything from tea to coffee. When using bark, only get it from newly cut tree trunks, it is the tannins within it that you are after so don't use trunks that have been lying for ages. The process I use to extract the dye is to boil the bark, grass etc in water for about 2 hours replacing the water as it evaporate – the longer you boil it the more concentrated the dye will be. Once finished sieve the remains of the material out of the dye into a large bucket and into this you place your rawhide in strips or whole. Leather such as yeg-tan leather is made like this from the tannins of bark after being suspended in them for months at a time. But that process is complex, all you need to do here is allow the colour produced to soak into the hide a little, although I have left rawhide in dyes for upto 2 weeks producing a hide slightly thicker, softer and having leather like texture.

Even if the tiller goes all wrong or a limb breaks and cracks you on the nose, your still left with some very good kindling!!!

Making a flat bow from timber.

There are alot of bow courses and books from which you can learn alot more then what's written here, but I have tried to set out a few of the basic stages in making a bow from timber.

To start with most species of wood can be used, both hard and soft wood in making a bow. I have experimented with many of them and experimenting is the best way to learn any skill.

selection of wood and marking out bow, initial or floor tillering, backing with rawhide, final tillering and polish, and lastly other backing system for weak tillers or strengthen soft woods.

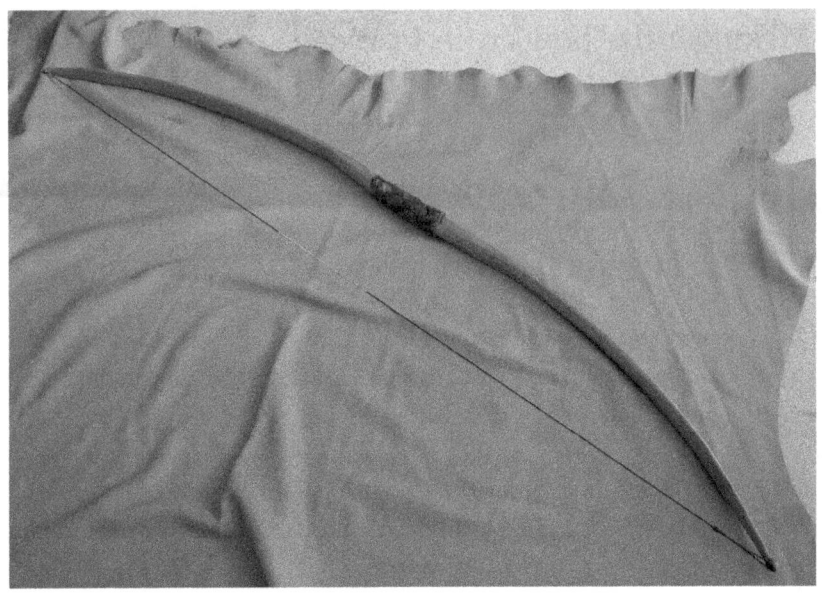

Picture above is of an old rectangular rawhide backed flat bow I made from a slice of oak taken off of a door from my local joiners shop. Dimensions are 5 foot 10 inches long, 1 ½ inches wide over all tapering 5 inches from the ends to ½ inch nicks. 6 inch long handle, height 1 inch tapering for 5 inches either side to ½ inch, which is the depth along the entire length of both limbs from handle to the start of the nocks where as the width narrowed I left slightly more depth. The bow was 50lb at 28 inch long arrows to start with but over 5 years of use has dropped to 35lb. Shooting at 45 angle, the furthest it shot a homemade 30 inch arrow was 120m – it is very light and easy to string.

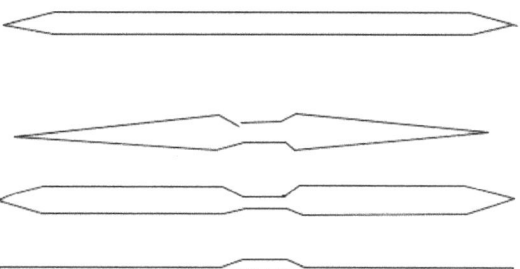

More common flat bow shapes made with sawn wood, dimensions are personnal preferance but I noramly stick to about 6 foot high, 2 inches wide (2 1/2 for top bow shape) narrowing to 1/2 inch at nocks - 6 inches for handle of about 1 1/3 inches wide - hight of it depends if you want the bow to bernd at the handle or not - just a MM higher if you do want it to bend at the handle, higher to stop this - better to leave it high then cut when tillering.

Timber selection and marking out bows dimensions

- Making a bow out of timber is a different kettle of fish to making one out of yew, or a stave. Any cuts made by an axe or drawknife tend to follow the growth ring rather then cut across it (with lemonwood being an exception), making it easy to mess up as shown above while I was trying to cut out the wood towards the nock. This is said to be due to the drying process – timbers are normally heat dried whereas most timber gathered from fallen trees is naturally dried thus ensuring better preservation of the cells/fibres that make up the wood. Heat treatment tends to destroy these cells and fibres to a higher degree; taking away some of the power and flexing capabilities of the wood – hence why most high powered timber bows are laminated out of different woods to improve strength and use of each different wood characteristic.

To help prevent the messing up as shown above, I also use a rasp and other files as shown in this photo. For those unused to using an axe it would be a better alternative. For this reason I always try to get timber from hardwood suppliers or the joiner as near to the dimensions of the bow as possible as this cuts down on the hard work i.e. the dimensions of the timber for the oak bow on page one was 6 foot long, 1 ½ wide, 1 inch depth. Also most important is to ensure that the growth rings are running fairly straight from top to bottom on the wider side. Of course, power tools can always be used but remember as well as getting the job done quicker, they can also mess up the whole bow quicker also!!!

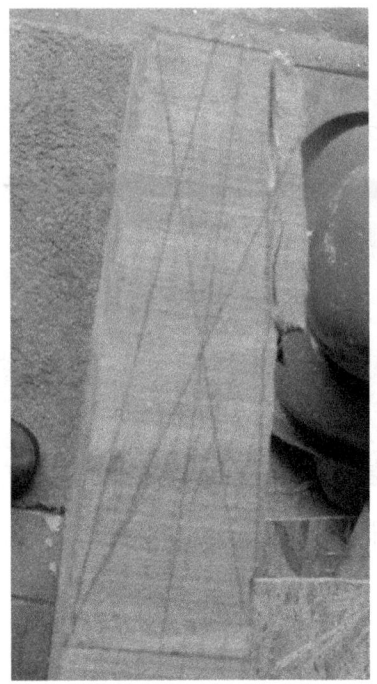 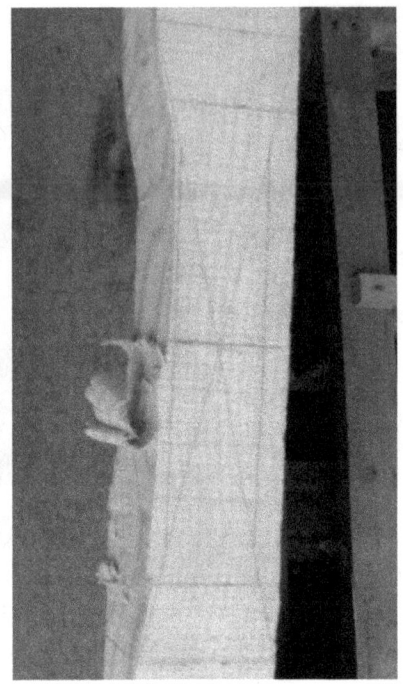

Once you have the timber the next thing to do is mark out for the self nocks (made from the wood and not horn etc) and handles to the dimension you desire – ensure you cut the ends an inch or so longer then you want to help prevent splitting, plus gives room for mistakes. You can see above how I cut the handle with an axe by cutting from the ends into the middle, this helps prevent cutting into the wood which could happen cutting from the middle towards the nocks.

Chopping away (or rasping) and initial or floor tillering

- The next job is possibly the most difficult and that is to cut out the belly (the side of the bow that faces you). The amount you take off here dictates the power of the limbs and bow, plus each limb has to have equal amounts taken off each side in order to produce an evenly tillered bow. For now I normally just take enough off to start the limbs bending. It might help to mark down the bow to the depth you wish to cut. For the oak bow I planned to go from (the handle) 1 inch to ½ inch depth limbs (nocks), so not alot and made a mark from the back of the bow of 5/8 of an inch (5/8's being the depth left at the nock end where the width narrowed). I used a camp axe to remove large amounts of wood and the mini axe for smaller detailed amounts but this takes experience, you could either choose to gain some or use the rasp. The photo's above shows me chopping around the handle area, but having already finished the initial wood removal from the bottom limb the bow did tend to vibrate alot as I removed wood – this is where it may be better to place into a vice or clamp of some sort to continue.

The above photo demonstrates initial tillering, which is checking for a bend in a limb and that the shape of the bend or curve on both limbs are similar. Above you can see that one is obviously flexing more than the other meaning that the stiffer limb needs more wood removed. Once you start this sort of testing of the bow or tillering, *Remove* only small slivers of wood. As the saying states 'you can always remove wood but you can't put it back' so from here on in, take your time; do little then check – it is also advisable to flex the limbs a few times after removing any amount of timber as the wood may take some time to show any difference.

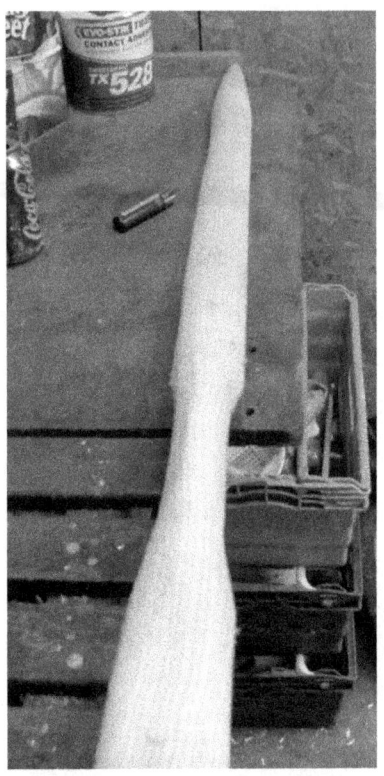

Before the next stage of tillering can occur, nocks have to be cut into the top of each limb, some people do temporary one's then cut out or attach horn etc once tillering has finished but I just used the one. You can cut any sort of nock you want as long as it serves the purpose of holding the string in place. You can cut all around from back (side of bow facing away from you) and belly or just the sides of the stave. Experiment and see which is best for you. After this, round up the limbs to make a more D profile and handle can be done with the rasp and file.

Backing with rawhide – I normally back my bows in rawhide which I make myself, you can buy it which is probably a better idea but do not use dog chews or white bleached rawhide – the additives in them make them weak, good for drum heads etc but not on bows or for braiding. Being a flat backed bow the method used is pretty much shown in the photo above and on the next page. Just damp the rawhide and apply glue (I use epoxy) to the bow and rawhide then fix as shown over the page.

After you have glued the rawhide use a metal scraper or other sort of blunt edge to ease out any air bubbles trapped between the rawhide and bow, then fix on wood blanks and clamps. I normally only do one side of the bow at a time but if you have the tools available there is no harm in doing the whole bow in one sitting. Once clamped, leave for about 3 to 5 days to set then remove the clamps and trim rawhide. Once the bow is tillererd and smoothed, paint on some varnish (I use yacht varnish) to avoid the rawhide getting damp. Apply about three coats sanding down each with the wire wool – this will then produce a smooth surface.

Figure 6

Final Tiller and Polishing – (leave tillering till a week after backing is applied)

The final stage of tillering is the most skilled part of making a self bow and involves using two pieces of essential equipment. First being a solid thin, long piece of wood with grooves cut out of it at spaces of 1 inch starting from 10 inches from the end to 30 inches. The second should include (but not shown) a wide, thin piece of wood with U shape cut out of the top of it attached 5 -6 feet up a wall (wide enough to accommodate the handle of a bow and deep enough to ensure it stays in place) with a pulley attached in the same wall directly underneath it at just above floor level (a marked grid on the wall behind helps to judge curve). Plus I use what I call a tillering string which is made extra thick from Dacron (24 ply instead of 12). The stick is mainly an aid when testing strength of bow by setting up as shown then without releasing the string from the groove taking the strain of it with a weighting devise of some sort (I use the kind fisherman use with a hook one end) . Plus it serves to help you to look at the bow more carefully to judge it's tiller or even take photos of it. The pulley devise is where most of the work occurs. After the floor tiller is over attach the tillering string and place the bow in the wood fixed into the wall, then attach another string from the along that string directly underneath the centre of the bow, play it through the pulley and walk back. The purpose of this is so you can first pull the bow a few times (allowing the bow to compensate for any wood removed) and judge where any needs to be removed. In figure 6 it is obvious that although the right limb is fairly even in the way it bends, the left one bends more near the handle then has no bend from the mid section to the nock. You only remove wood where it does not bend, so it would mean that a little should be removed from the left mid section to the nock. When I say a little, I mean that you may have to only use sand paper. The most essential thing to do is re-test the tiller after every small piece of wood removed. It takes time and you may ruin it a few times, I did and still do after not making one for awhile.

When you're happy with the tillering, the bow can have its final sanding. I use very fine 180 grit then wet the bow and run the wire wool over it repeating this about three times (this gets rid of very fine fibres) . Then I rub a stone over it all (except for the back – leave this semi rough to take the backing if you want one) which serves to compound the wood after the wetting and brings the wood upto a very nice sheen. Once the bow is tillererd and smoothed, paint on some varnish (I use yacht varnish) to avoid the rawhide getting damp. Apply about three coats sanding down each with the wire wool – this will then produce a smooth surface.

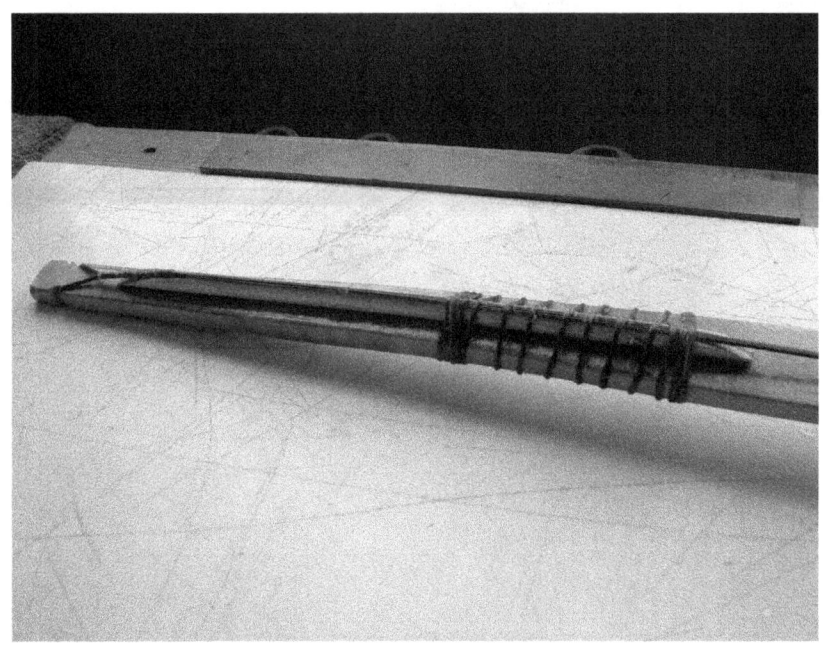

Additional methods to overcome problem tillers (weak spots) or to strengthen soft woods – backing with rawhide is just one way to help protect the back of a bow or help strengthen it, although laminating on another piece of wood is better for this then rawhide, lemonwood is especially good for this and readily available. Bows like the yew bow have their own excellent backing in the form of sap wood against the heart wood. Above I show two methods I have used to help strengthen and adjust for badly cut or tillered bows plus are especially good when using soft wood. The first is running string between the nocks along the entire length of the bow, these are best attached while having the back arced in a concave shape so tighten up when the bow is strung – all you have to do is ensure that you run the string through a tube of some sort by the handle to stop it rubbing the handle covering or your hands. The second method shown was to compensate for a severe change in direction of the growth rings, rather

than running nock to nock, they went side to side in the area shown. Attaching the extra piece of beading (could use anything that does the job) strengthened that part of the limb and evened up the tiller

Attaching string under handle wrap.

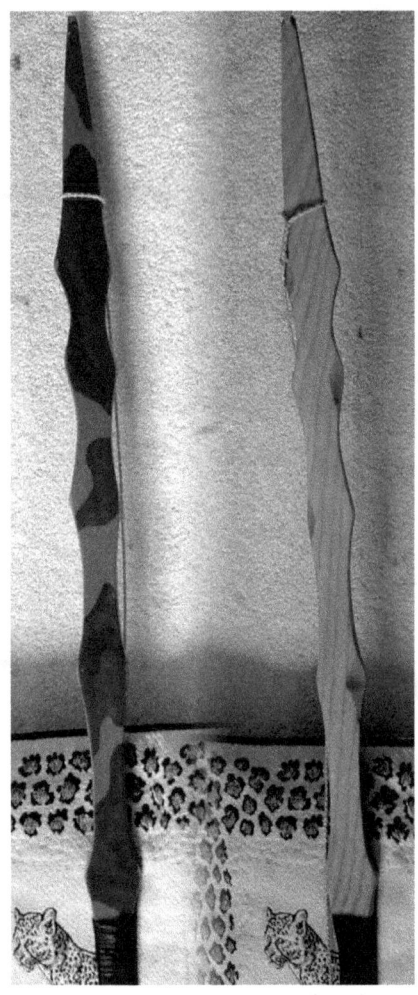

An example of creative persuasion from kids brought about this design – made from ash it is only 5 foot long 2 ½ inches wide and is only 25lb but really tested my tillering skills.

Making Arrows and bow strings

There is a wide selection of readymade and pre-cut arrow kits which can be bought from archery supply places, but I still prefer to make my own, it completes the pleasure of making all my archery equipment.

The arrows I describe here have been used on bows upto 65lb. They are primarily for everyday use and practise.

 Arrows - shafts sizes and making the nock, paint/decorations, points, fletching, attaching fletch.

Bow strings – string jig, setting up string, making end loops and serving, reverse twisting Dacron string.

Batches of arrows nocked and painted, ready for fletching.

Arrows

Shaft sizes and nocks – I normally use 9mm or 11/36th of an inch beading from the hardware store for the shafts, which I cut to length (normally 30 inches) by first scoring or sawing around the beading then snapping off. This prevents the beading from splitting. To make them straight I soak them in hot water and then fix to a rigid core and leave for a day to dry. It does not produce a perfect job but good enough for practise arrows. Next job is to make the nocks, for this I use the round, oval and triangle profile needle files to produce a shape as shown on the next page. Start by making a mark across the top of the shaft then use the triangle file to make a V into the shaft. Next use the oval file and file 5mm down from the base of the V, lastly using the circular file at the bottom of this cut, as shown in figure 7 to produce a nock that can grip the string (based on 12 ply dacron string with serving). I developed this for kids to stop the arrow falling out of the string while nocking the arrow; it also strengthens the shaft cutting down on splitting.

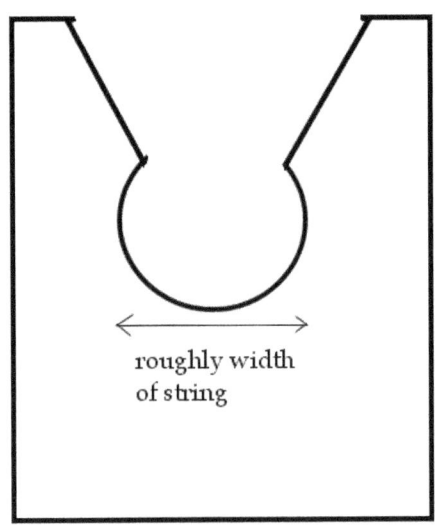

Figure 7

Paint and decorating – Before painting you may have to smooth the shaft – this can be done with rubbing it with wire wool. You do not have to paint the shafts but I find it an easy way to help guide the positioning of the fletching and identification of separate sets. You could use either oil paint or coloured tape. First I use masking tape to mark off the parts I am going to paint then paint and leave for 2 hours or so till dry. Once dry remove the taps and rub over the shaft again to remove the bur of the paint it also further compresses and smooth's the shaft.

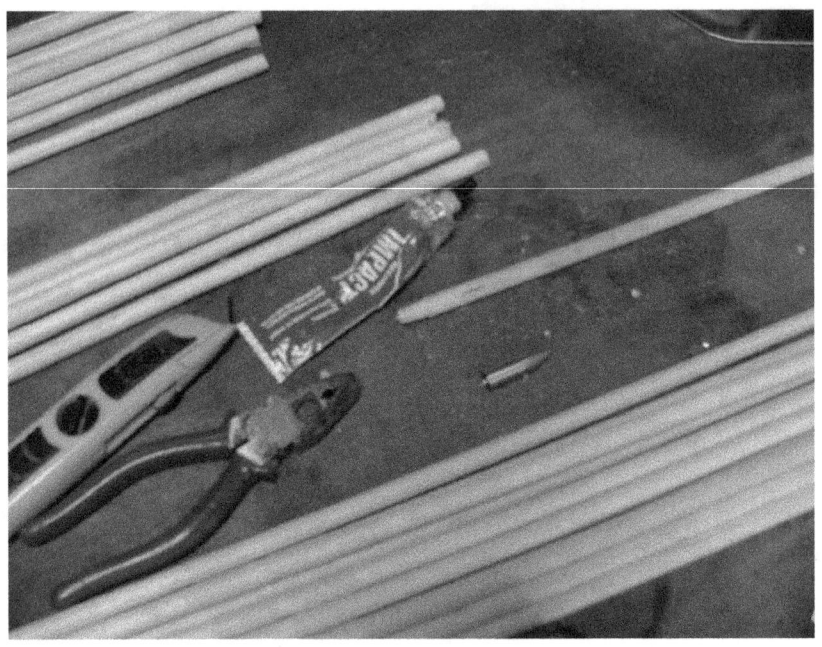

Points — When ordering points, bear in mind the width of the shaft you are using (beading is normally 11/36th whereas shaft from an archery supplier can be 11/36th or 5/16th). Apart from coming in different widths and weights (I normally gets the lightest) they are also available in either tapered or screw on fits. The tapers are easily fitted by using a special pencil sharpening type of cutter which carves/tapers the end of the shaft to fit into the points. The screw on points needs to have the end of the shaft sanded down to 7.5mm diameter (based on an original width of 9mm) this ensures a smooth transition between the point and the shaft. I do this by first scoring around the shaft ¾ inch from the end of the shaft as shown above and then sanding down slowly until the desired width is achieved. I use epoxy glue to affix both types of points onto the shaft, it is not the best but it works. Regardless of the type of point you use, after shooting an arrow make sure that you mentally mark the spot where the arrow is in the target so that if upon pulling it out the point has come off, you know where it is to pull or push it out.

Fletch – Fletching are available either bought from a supplier or I prefer to collect mine (Turkey near Xmas, pheasants' in October, falcons in autumn or from just the woods/fields etc). The photo above slows a variety of feathers that I collected, the larger being the turkey plus a few from pigeons, falcons and even a snowy owl, plus the yellow and small triangle shaped black ones are bought ones.

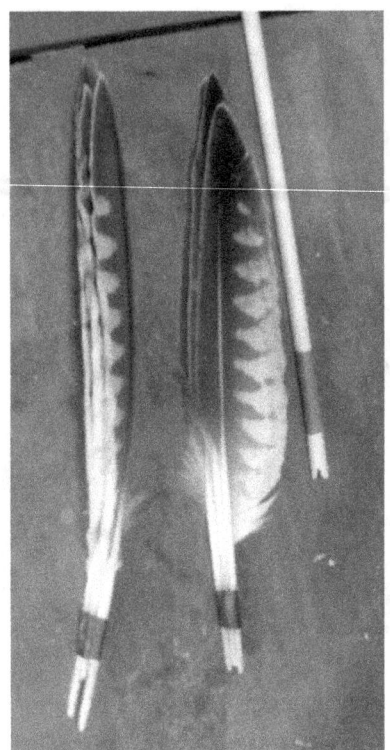 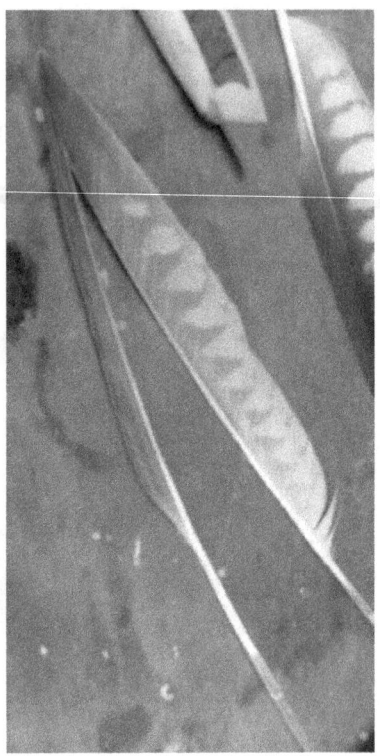

In regards to collected fletching, I first put them into groups of three as shown above, this is to later produce 3 matching sized and angled fletching for one arrow. To split both sides of the feather as shown above right, first gently tap along the length of the spine, then using a sharp knife cut down the middle of its length starting from the thicker end taking extra care towards the narrow end.

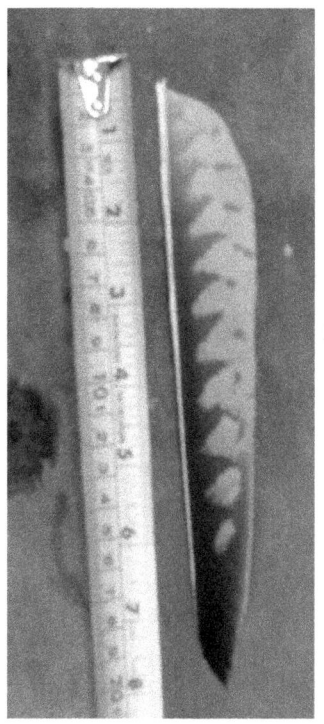
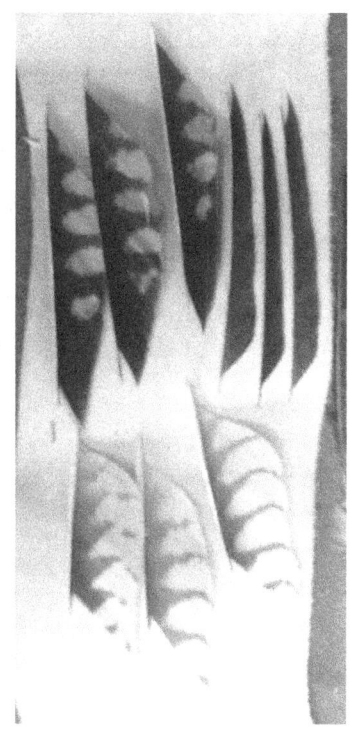

Attaching fletch – The amount of fletching you could get from one side of a feather depends on the length of fletching you need. I try to get as many as I can get from my feathers. When you do cut remember to add 2 inches, which is for the 1 inch of exposed spine you leave either side of the feather which you need to attach the feather to the arrow. Once cut, simply use a pair of scissors to cut away the barbs and expose the spine. At this stage you can also trim along the top of the barbs to any shape. It is also important to gently sand the underside of the spine you cut into to create a smooth flat surface.

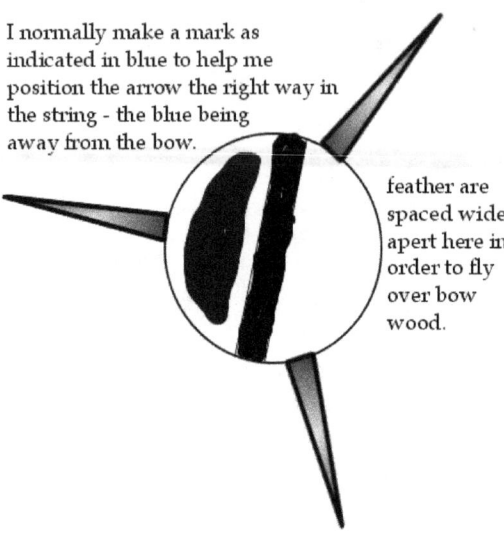

I normally make a mark as indicated in blue to help me position the arrow the right way in the string - the blue being away from the bow.

feather are spaced wide apert here in order to fly over bow wood.

Figure 8 – method for attachment marking for string

The positioning of the feather onto the shaft is important, as shown above in order to ensure that it flows over the wood of the bow without being pushed off its line of flight, plus ensure that the flow of the barbs curve towards the nock end of the shaft. If you are using bought fletching I normally just glue these into place but with the collected ones, due to their nature they have to be glued and tied into place to ensure they are aligned (although they can be left twisted which makes the arrow spin in flight). I start by applying glue to the top of the shaft and spine of the feathers then fix into place starting from the nock end first ensuring that the ends of the exposed spine are just under the bottom of the nock. Once all three are attached you then need to serve or whip over the exposed spine top and bottom (I use artificial sinew) which is covered in the string section. Applying a good solid serving at the top also strengthens the nock further.

I normally mark the end of the shaft to help guide me placing the arrows in the bow string, when using bought feathers you can just use a different colour fletching for the same purpose. Once the Arrows are finished smooth the shaft again with wire wool and a stone and apply either varnish or wood polish and enjoy.

String

String Jig — This is the jig I use to make my strings on — it is simply a scrap piece of mahogany 6 ½ feet long by 2 inches wide. As can be seen one end has a series of holes with the other having a long groove which is used to pull the string tight once applied as below.

Setting up jig - smaller pieces of wood like above are placed on both ends with nails attached to their ends (could be anything attached but ensure the metal is smooth so that the string is not damaged) and a hole made in the middle – I used a coach bolt to attach to the longer piece of wood. For this example I am making a 12 ply string out of black and white Dacron waxed thread (this is strong enough for upto 80lb bow). The normal gauge in making string is that it should be made about 3 inches shorter than the length of the nock's on your bow but I have found with my jig that making the string 4 – 5 inches shorter than the bow nocks is sufficient in producing a string that long enough to produce the 6 inch gap between the string and handle of the bow once strung. Once made, fine adjustments can be made to shorten the length at any time by twisting the string. To start making your bow string the end pieces of wood should be set as shown above; in line with one another. Then starting at one nail wind the string between them 6 times keeping it tight all the time and tie off, the other string should be wound from the other end to ensure that there is a tying knot at each end and not bunched together which would cause undue wear around it when strung.

Next very carefully open out the two end pieces of wood as shown above ensuring that the knots are off centre.

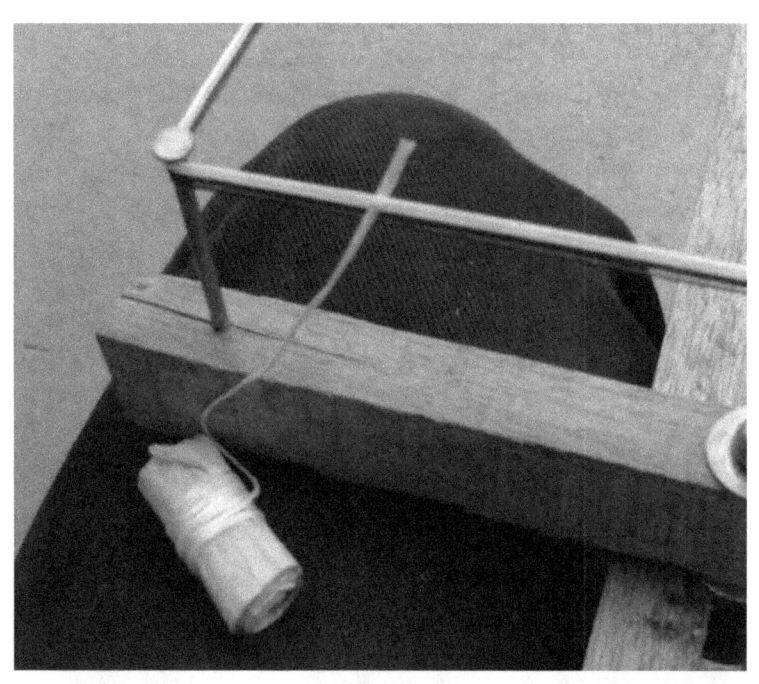
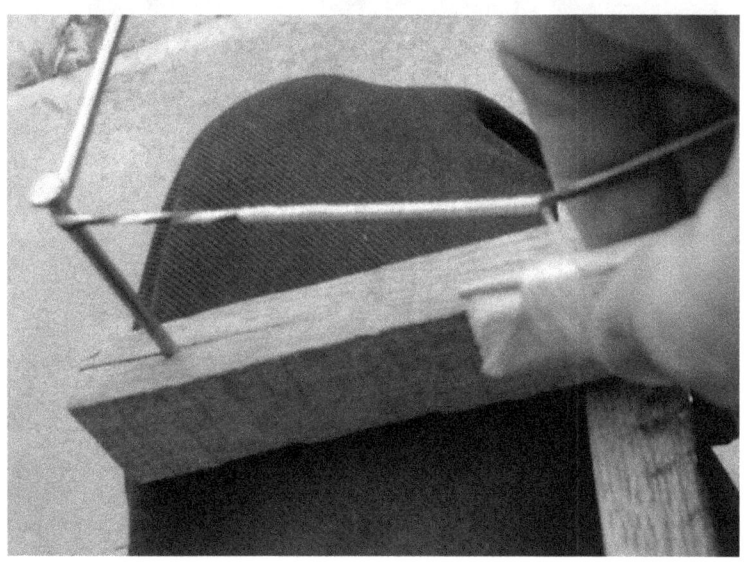

Making end loops and serving – What we do next is the serving also called whipping for the end loops. To start I wind a long length of thread around a piece of beading or rolled cardboard, next beginning a short way from one nail place the end of it through the middle of the strings. Then wind the thread around the string as shown on the previous page ensuring not only to cover the short piece you threaded through the string but mostly that the string is evenly covered by the thread. Continue doing this until you are 3 – 4 inches away from the other nail – take care that the knot is totally covered by thread.

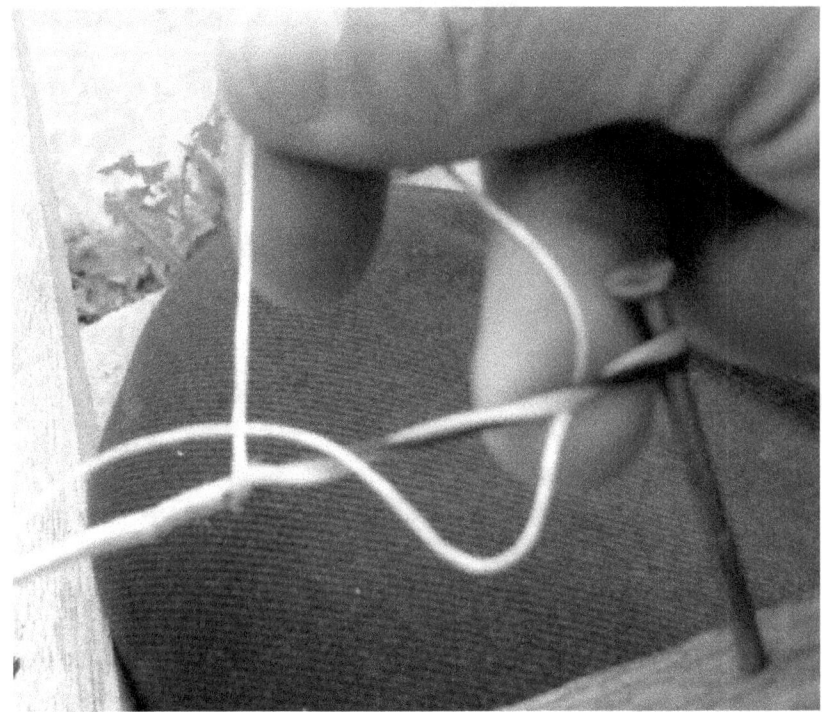

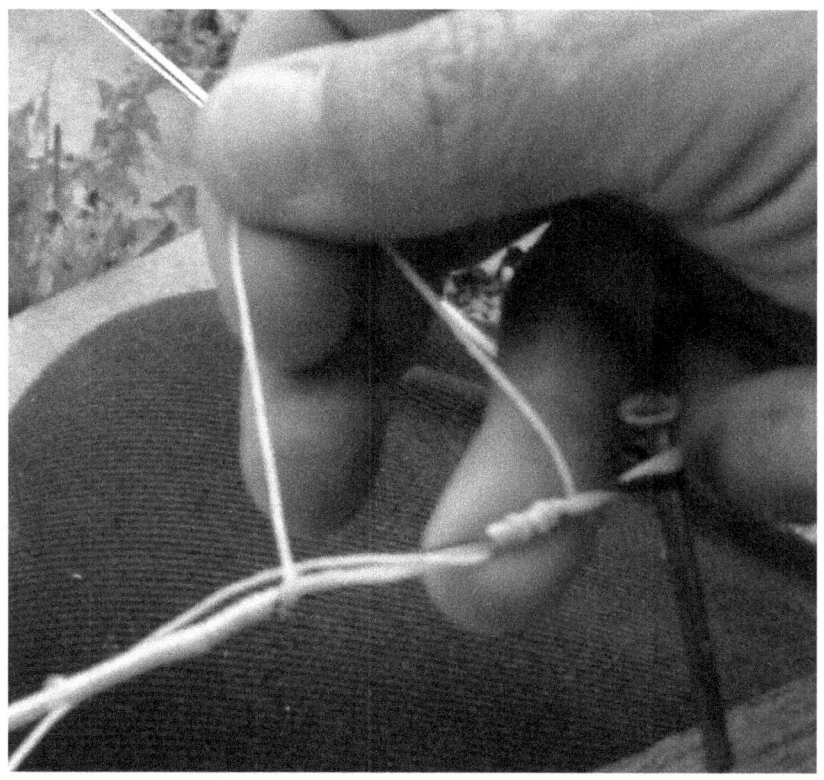

The method for ending the serving depends of the direction you have wound the thread thus far, in the above photo's the thread was wound under towards you and over the top. To start the end do one run of under then run it back over/ under, pull the thread up as shown above and place the thread under the standing thread (this being the vertical thread). Above right illustrates that you now wind the thread round the string in the opposite direction – do this for upto 12 turns ensuring that the end finishes under the standing thread. Next take the standing thread and carry on winding it towards the nail ensuring it is tight as you wind. When you have wound it the 12 turns pull the loose end. Do the same for the other end of the string. This serving will rest on the nocks of the bow.

Once each end has had its nock serving done, place the end pieces of wood back into the positions they were in when you first attached the string. Now you will apply more serving to close the loops for your bow nocks – ensure that the loops will be wide enough to fit onto the nocks and that you serve a good few inches past the nock serving you just did – I normally make one end wider than the other to aid in stringing the bow. After the loops have been finished you can take it off the jig and check the length, if it is too long then just place one loop into the jig and twist a few times until you are happy with the length. Finally serve the middle of the string; this is to protect the string from the arrows. I normally find the centre of the string and starting 5 inches from it, serving for 5 inches past the centre to the other side.

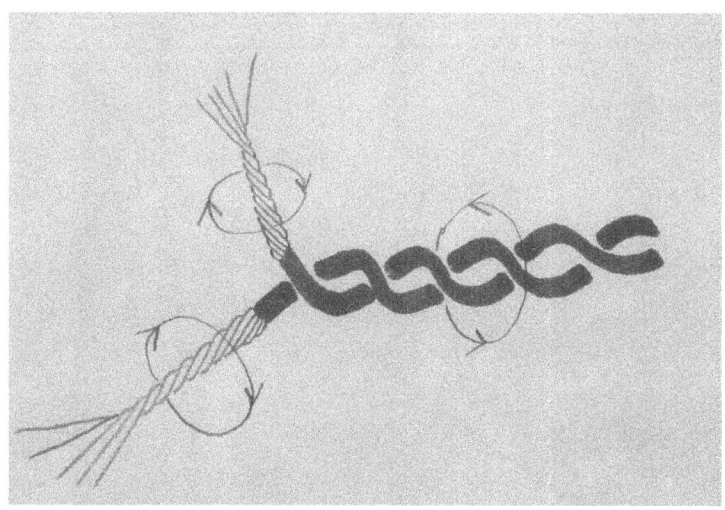

Reverse twisting bow string – many people find the method for reverse twisting duffercult because it involves twisting string one way and then another at the same time but after practise it gets easier. The method for 12 ply bow string it to grasp two runs of loose string, 6 threads in each, then as shown above twist the upper bundle left to right while twisting it under the other bundle right to left. To see if you have it right after a few turns, let go of the string – if it unravels then you've done it wrong, if it does not, then you've done it right.

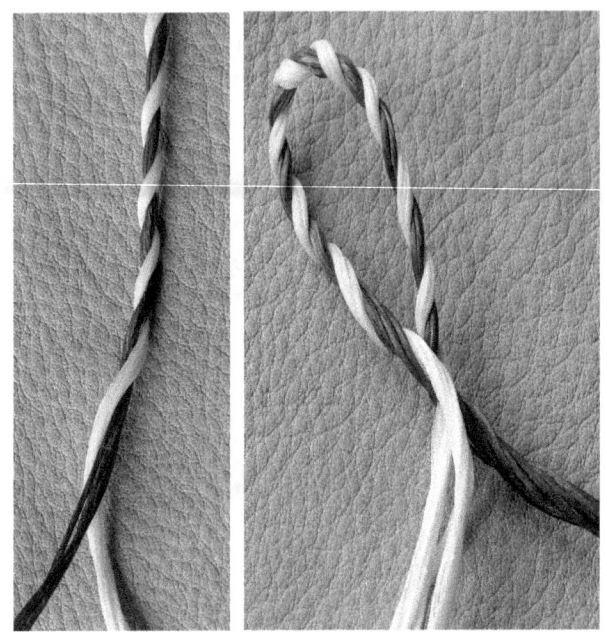

For a 12 ply bow string you need to cut 12 lengths of string 1 ¾ times longer than the bow, then starting at the middle of these, begin the reverse twisting. Do this for about 5 -6 inches and make a loop as shown above middle, bring the strings together and start reverse twisting again. The aim is to make a string about 14 inches longer then the bow; once this is achieved you can tie off the strings and/or burning the ends together.

On those odd occasions when you just can't find the arrow – look up!!!!!

Resources

Supplies;

Flybow shop - Got loads of equipment and materials for flat, long and recurve bows.

Highland Horn – supplies for recurves, arrows and stick making.

Ebay – great place to pick up used or new inexpensive drawknives and axes (can be any make as long as they are sharp) plus bow making staves and other archery supplies – not liked by many but I find it the safest most secure and easiest place to buy things.

Richard head longbow – good for bow making, arrow supplies.

Books;

Traditional bowyer's bibles - 4 volumes – probably the best books around which cover everything you need to know about making all sorts of bow types.

Forums;

BCUK – mainly a forum about bush craft but also has bow making members.

Paleoplanet – has more in-depth discussions and tutorials for bow makers.

Courses;

Woodsmoke – Bush craft and outdoor skills company been running for over 10 years – holds many other great courses.

www.ingramcontent.com/pod-product-compliance
Lightning Source LLC
Chambersburg PA
CBHW061248040426
42444CB00010B/2302